T0198826

We're Three
A Story About Families and The Only Child

Order this book online at www.trafford.com
or email orders@trafford.com

Most Trafford titles are also available at major online book retailers.

Text © Copyright 2008, 2011 by Vivian Cameron-Gallo
Illustrations © Copyright 2008 Christina Simcic.

All rights reserved. No part of this publication may be reproduced, stored in a retrieval system, or transmitted, in any form or by any means, electronic, mechanical, photocopying, recording, or otherwise, without the written prior permission of the author.

Note for Librarians: A cataloging record for this book is available from Library and Archives Canada at www.collectionscanada.ca/amicus/index-e.html

PRINT INFORMATION AVAILABLE ON THE LAST PAGE.

ISBN: 978-1-4251-7215-2 (sc)
ISBN: 978-1-4669-3245-6 (e)

Trafford rev. 08/30/2018

Trafford
PUBLISHING®

www.trafford.com
North America & international
toll-free: 1 888 232 4444 (USA & Canada)
fax: 812 355 4082

We're Three

A Story About Families and The Only Child

Written by Vivian Cameron-Gallo
and illustrated by Christina Simcic

Dedication

If you are an only child and holding this book you should know this book has been written for you! I dedicate this book to my inspiration, my daughter Ava, and to my loving husband Anthony. Special thanks to my sister, Valerie for editing and to all our friends and famiy who critiqued the pages in their process.

-VCG

With all my love I dedicate this book to all the "only" children and grown-ups, who have enriched my life with their presence and inspiried me to work on this book. You all have your own place in my heart, Daniel, Alexandra, Ava, Lukas, and Rosalie, to name just a few dear to my heart.

-CS

About the Author

Vivian Cameron-Gallo lives in Westchester County, NY. She was inspired to write this book by her own family of three and in particular her wonderful daughter. This is her first book and she plans on many more to come.

She works as a freelance interior display designer and enjoys gardening and yoga.

About the Illustrator

Christina Simcic lives and creates in Westchester County, NY. She is a dedicated mural artist, always eager to discover new artistic ways of expression and to improve her knowledge and skills. Illustrating this book gave her the opportunity to play with the color pencils that kids too, love so much. You are welcome to visit Christina's website at www.maisoncappellari.com

There are all kinds of families

We are

in this great message

EARTH

Some are big and some are little...

with lots of family...

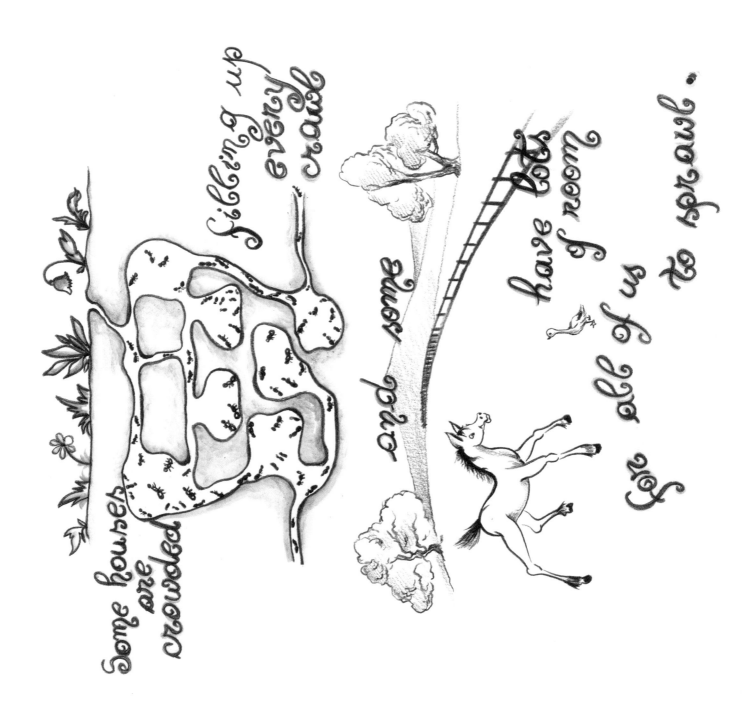

Draw your house here

In my house there is just the right fit.

There's a Mommy plus a Daddy plus one more ... plus a lot.

There's the love ♥ that we share and the fun that we have that we play everywhere !!! and hope that we play that we games with ♥ The games !!!

We're the perfect line up

Tic Tac Toe...

And that's something I thought you should know

Ring-a-Rosie is perfect for 3 ...

You

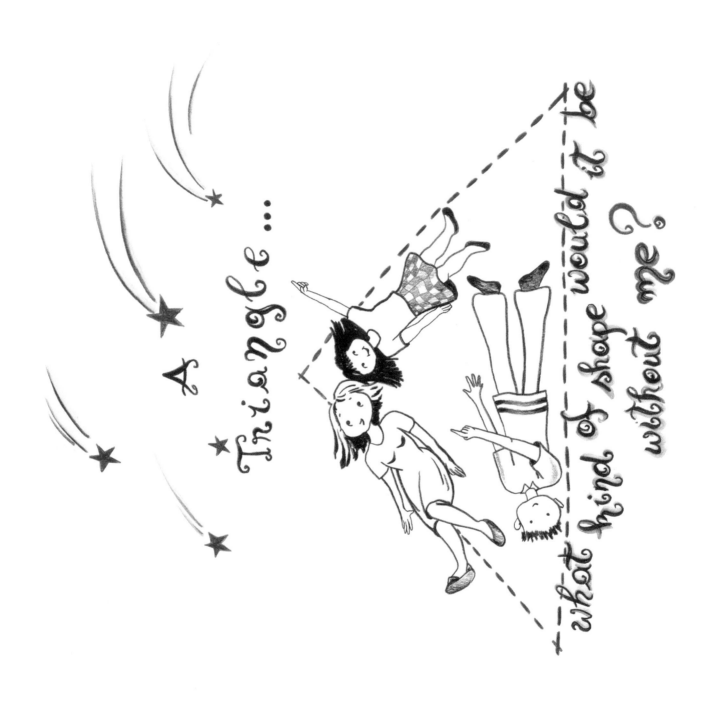

A Triangle ...

what kind of shape would it be without me?

I hope we're more than

Draw things that you do with your family.

If the circle of my family

I am a great find!

So...

What about you?

Draw your family here!

We're Three!

There are all kinds of families in this great big world.
Some are big with lots of kids...and some are small,
with not too many, or simply none at all.

Some houses are crowed filling up every crawl
and some have lots of room for all of us to sprawl.
In my house there's just the right fit!
There's a Mommy and Daddy and one more bit.

There's the love that we share and the fun that we have
with the games that we play everywhere. We're the
perfect line up for Tic Tac Toe and that's something
I thought you should know! Ring-a-Rosie is perfect for 3...
A Triangle...what kind of shape would it be without me?

In the circle of my family, I'm a great find!
We're a family of three and I'm one of a kind!

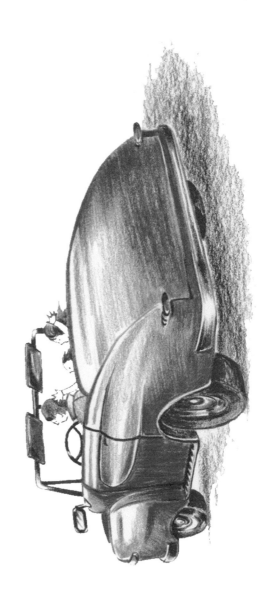

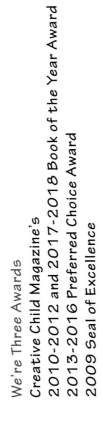

We're Three Awards
Creative Child Magazine's
2010-2012 and 2017-2018 Book of the Year Award
2013-2016 Preferred Choice Award
2009 Seal of Excellence

Visit our interactive virtual lounge at:
www.onlychildkidsclub.com/lounge.htm

For printable copies of the blank pages in the book go to:
http://www.onlychildkidsclub.com/Links.html

Printed in the United States
By Bookmasters